The Kingdom of God

By José A. Claudio Bonilla

Dedication

Jesus said to him, "I tell you the truth, today you will be with me in paradise (Luke 23: 43 NIV)

Addressing these words has been a little difficult for me. Thinking about health issues, illness, cancer, pain, tests, surgical procedures, and discomfort among many other struggles that a person I have in mind has experienced, makes me sad, anxious, and sometimes helpless -looking at a distance how this woman of God debilitates while family and relatives wait for that moment when Jesus call her to paradise. I cannot dedicate this book to another person but to my sister Irma, one of our members of the Kingdom of God. I love you, sister!

Acknowledgments

The Kingdom of God is here, at hand! It has been here! It will be here, in heaven, and for eternity! Thanks be to God for all the people, teaching, and activities that in one way or another invested and motivated me to meet the conditions to enter the Kingdom of God: repentance from sin and build a Christian character; believing in the Gospel - believing the Christian message; recognize Jesus Christ's sacrifice - to live eternally; acknowledge baptism - in the name of the Father, Son, and Holy Spirit; acknowledge the necessity of God's Holy Spirit in me, and join the family of believers - Christ's church.

My marked path to enter God's kingdom has come accompanied by the teaching, motivation, and encouragement of my parents and siblings since childhood. Baseball, softball, and volleyball, but, particularly the rules of softball "forced" me to participate in Christ's church. Pastors, church leaders, seminarians, university professors, and community organizers, have empowered me with evangelism and organizing/ advocacy strategies to search and "see light at the end of a tunnel." Common good for everyone!

Introduction

If anyone talks about social justice based instruction, first one's instruction must be based on social justice education and justice-affirming experience! Also, a faith-based experience and practice, of course, will bring faith, social values, belief, and religious leadership into the public arena. But above all, the voice and presence of God among those activists who advocate for the common-good of any particular community. This is the case of the one writing this manuscript. Inspired by Jesus Christ's ministry on earth while offering the kingdom of God and an education with a foundation of more than 200 years ago, I, José A. Claudio Bonilla, the writer, articulate social concerns with the Gospel. One of my experiences with social justice, which has empowered the presentation of this work, comes from my years as a student in the Colgate Rochester Crozer Divinity School-Master of Divinity Program. As many readers may learn, Colgate "has served as one of the world's leading progressive theological schools, preparing socially conscious, socially active leaders who impact the world through Christ-centered leadership and service." Throughout the school's printed history, two faculty members have been focused as leaders prepared and equipped to participate in social changes faith-based: "Walter Rauschenbusch (1861-1918), the founder of the Social Gospel movement of the late 19th century" and Dr. Martin Luther King, Jr. (1951), who graduated from Crozer.

The second one, a few years later, would put to use the social ethics he had been taught at Crozer and lead the emergent Civil Rights Movement that would change forever the character of American society"
(https://www.crcds.edu/history). It was there at Colgate that I acquired experience in implementing social justice based interpretation, writing, instruction, and practice when the Holy Spirit called and inspired me to actively advocate for justice.

Life at Colgate opened a door for me, which I was not expecting or even could not imagine – a world of inclusion and affirmation, human and cultural diversity, pluralism, sexual orientation, and gender identity understanding. All though I am an exclusive Christian in faith and belief (and with the help of the Holy Spirit, that will never change), this door has been my entrance to an inclusive, diverse, and progressive ministry. As President Barack Obama always says, "The world is changing and it is necessary that we change with it."

The door to an inclusive ministry filled with social justice began while experiencing Colgate during the pastoral ministry internship. Being a Christian practicing Christianity in one of the Churches that honor the cross and the flame- The United Methodist Church (UMC), it was God's will that I gained experience in an open and affirming congregation (ONA). This is a congregation that enters into full ministry with the Lesbian, Gay, Bisexual, and Transgender

Community (LGBT). Now, there was a heterosexual minister, rigid in Christian theology, and with conservative Christian educational roods serving in what many of my Latino colleagues call "a gay church." Because I was serving in such a congregation, the majority of the people I conducted one-on-one with used to ask me, "Do you have a family member who is gay…?" My response most times was, "Why don't you ask me straight forward," "Are you gay?" "No. I am not gay! But I would like to treat every human being with dignity and respect." This teaching and ministerial serving experience empowered my vision and practice of social justice in any educational setting.

My third experience with justice practices, which I consider to be meaningful while exploring the Gospel about to be studied and advocacy, articulates the second one. This experience came full of power, the power taught by Gamaliel Foundation in Chicago, Illinois. This was while serving in the ONA congregation- an experience with community organizing. Here, my ministry began to make more sense- community effectiveness, political and environmental involvement, and social and economic participation. Here, I entered ministry with human lives in a dimension that I had never experienced before, considering individual and community needs. This experience helped me in a great magnitude to articulate the Christian faith, and the world of the Bible with social concerns. This is one of the reasons I am exploring and sharing Jesus' ministry in the Gospel of Luke while offering the kingdom of God.

Throughout my experience in Gamaliel, a faith-based organization that provides training and consultation and develops the national strategy for its affiliated congregation-based community organizations, I met Gregory Galluzzo (Greg)-an oriented and focus person on community organizing

(https://en.wikipedia.org   /wiki/Gamaliel_Foundation). Greg personally went from Chicago to Buffalo, New York, to the congregation in which I was serving to assist and motivate me as a community leader to be a community organizer. Here I learned to organize people and money and to implement community-organizing principles in the church's mission practice. The experience in Gamaliel motivated the congregation to create, maintain, and expand independent grassroots faith-based advocacy for justice. I became one of the Clergy caucus participants and another community leader trained by the Gamaliel Foundation as former President Barack Obama was trained in his younger years. Yes, Barack Obama was trained and worked as a community organizer with the Developing Community Project on the far South Side of Chicago (1985-1988). He was also a consultant and trainer for the Gamaliel Foundation (https://en.wikipedia.org/wiki/Gamaliel_Foundation).

Finally, the social justice experience that has empowered my community service took a new turn. This time in the classroom and with Language Learning and Leadership! Becoming a student of the Teaching Speakers of Other Languages (TESOL) Master Degree Program at SUNY Fredonia-University of New York was a new exploring task for me! There, as in the church, I could not put aside the social justice principles learned while at Colgate and as a Community Organizer within Gamaliel. Therefore, it was not hard for me to adapt the organizing, activism, and advocacy strategies to education. It was not an easy task, especially while performing the Master thesis research. But looking at Mahatma Gandy, Martin Luther King, Jr., Nelson Mandela, and other world activists as models, I created a social justice curriculum as my Master's thesis project and graduated with a Language Learning and Leadership Degree in May 2017.

A variety of courses that underlined education advocacy were meaningful and created a clear conscience in me to identify student, family, and community needs, which I consider essential for the examination and exposition of the Gospel about to be studied and the events surrounding its narrative. The most interesting, meaningful, and energetics of these courses were the ones taught by Dr. Kate Mahoney, which included- assessment and evaluation of students. This task was performed by the use of tables, especially the one known as the decision-making process called PUMI-an acronym for Purpose, Use, Method, Instrument, which can be used to better inform assessment decisions for bilingual children (https://channelviewpublications.wordpress.com/tag/pu mi/).

Dr. Mahoney is an associate professor for the TESOL program in the Department of Language, Learning, and Leadership at Fredonia. Dr. Mahoney's major works address the validity of using achievement and language proficiency test scores for Emergent Bilingual Learners (EBLs)... in Arizona and nationally. While teaching theory, methods, and clinically-based courses at Fredonia, which includes *Assessment and Evaluation of Emergent Bilingual Learners, Content Area ESL*, Dr. Mahoney inspired me to perform the needs assessments that I am presenting in the table ahead.

The following table headlines the *needs, citations* where such needs are found, some brief *comments* on the biblical narrative, and the actual *citation* where the biblical text can be located. The table contains 4 columns and 37 rows, which may serve as a guide for the readers to identify the needs I assessed while performing a hermeneutical study of the Gospel of Luke. I would like the readers to know that the needs identified in this study are not all the ones contained in the text, not contemporarily unique to a given situation, and that time and culture may shed a different light on the textual narrative. Of course, there is always room for the Holy Spirit to inspire us to see new light for additional comments. Its content is simply brief information about the kingdom of God offered when oppression is taking place… The literature that follows the table is headlined as "kingdom of God" accompanied by a number (1,2,3, etc.) underlining the citation. There are 28 numbers, which indicate that at least 28 times the word "kingdom" or the phrase "kingdom of God" appears in the Gospel. Let's enjoy it!

Needs Assessment in Luke-in Relation to the Kingdom of God Texts

Need	Citation	Comments	Kingdom of God Text
Childlessness	1:7; 18	Zachariah & Elizabeth – Elizabeth was not able to conceive, and both were advanced in age	His kingdom will have no end (1: 30-33)
Fear	1:12	Zachariah to the spiritual being	1: 30-33
Inability to speak	1:20	Do to unbelief (Zachariah)	1: 30-33
Feeling of disgrace or shame	1:25	Elizabeth's feelings	1: 30-33

Negative spiritual disturbance	4:33	…there was a man possessed by a demon	"I must preach de kingdom of God" (4:43)
Sickness/illness	4:38	Simon's mother-in-law was suffering from a high fever,	4:43
Sickness and more demonic influences	4:40-41	People in the community	4:43
Hunger, disability, other diseases, and impure spirits	6:1-5; 6-11; 18	Jesus' disciples plucked some head of grain; the man with the withered hand, and people from all over Judea came to hear Jesus and be healed	"…for your is the kingdom of God" (6:20-26)
Poverty	6:20	"Looking at Jesus' disciple"	6:20-26

Hunger	6:21	Jesus' disciple	6:20-26
Weeping	6:21	Jesus' disciples	
Haters, exclusion, verbal abuse, rejection	6:22	Jesus' disciples	6:20-26
Sin, communication	7:37-50; 8:4-15	Jesus forgave the sins of a sinful woman; and communicated the secrets of the parable of the sower to His disciples	8:1,10
Intentional lack of resources	9:3	Jesus' disciples	9:1-2, 6, 10
Need of Healing	9:10	"those" among the crowd	9:10
Lack of food	9:12-13	The crowd and Jesus' disciples	9:11
Lack of dwelling	9:58	Jesus	9: 59-62
Death	9:60	A man relative	9:59-62

Intentional lack of provisions and personal comfort	10:3-7; 9-11	The mission of the seventy	10: 9; 11
Lack of spiritual education (prayer)	11:1-2	Jesus' disciples	11:2
Lack of speech-demonic influences	11:14	A man who was mute	11:20
Physical difference (crippled by a spirit for 18 years)	13:11	A woman	13:18-19; 20-21
Abdominal swelling	14:2	A man in the house of a prominent	14:8-11; 23
Wealth and riches misuse	16:1-15; 16-31	Shrewd Manager and The Rick Man and Lazarus	16:16; 16-31
Sin	17: 6 (in relation to 13:19)	Other disciples and the apostles	17:1-6

Suffering, rejection	17:25	Jesus and "this generation"	17:20-21
Lack of Justice, faith, self-pride, rejection,	18:1-8; 9-13; 15-17	The apostles	18:15-17
Lack of sharing resources (wealth)	18:18-30	Members of the community	18:18-29
Lack of sharing resources (wealth)	18:18-30	This was Peter's response to Jesus' comment about a rich man to enter the kingdom of God	18:28-30
Growth disorder- short stature	19:3	Zacchaeus-He wanted to see who Jesus was, but because he was short, he could not see over the crowd	19:1-11

Poverty, war, uprisings (resistance, rebellion, revolt), natural disasters, famines, pestilences, persecution, imprisonment, betray, death, hate	21:4-31	The story of the widow vs. the rich and events before the final times	21:1-31
Betray, dispute, trials	22:4	Judas *betrayed* Jesus; *dispute* about which of them (Jesus' disciples) was considered to be the greatest; trials-Jesus	22:16; 24-17; 29-30
Difficult decisions/actions	23:26-43; 51	Crucifixion of Jesus; Joseph of Arimathea's thinking about what had happened to Jesus.	23:50-51

Identity arguments; manipulation	23:3; 36-38; 39-43	Pilate questioning Jesus kingship; a soldier trying to manipulate Jesus; One of the criminals "not fearing God…	23: 3, 42

The Kingdom of God 1

This manuscript portion is introduced in a similar fashion. The writer of the Gospel of Luke underlines the accounts to all those individuals who "love God"-Theophilus" (God lovers). It is my intention that you can identify accounts in which the "the kingdom of God" is presented and the events or stories surrounding such presentation. These accounts may not be pleasant for some of the characters involved in each story. They record certain kind of oppression that, in turn, creates pain, suffering, fear, and any other feeling, sensation, and emotion, which may become stumbling blocks for the characters to enjoy freedom. In this work, I have identified such oppressions as "needs," which will be "assessed" within the story or event in which Jesus' kingdom or the kingdom of God is presented and/or offered by Jesus…. For example, When the word *kingdom* is highlighted for the first time in the Gospel in relationship to Jesus and the preparedness of people to be ready for the Lord (1: 17, 33), there were some people being oppressed for any particular situation in life (Zechariah and Elisabeth). They were righteous before God, walking blamelessly in all the commandments and statutes of the Lord (1: 6). But they had no child because Elizabeth was barren, and both were advanced in years (1: 7). Apparently, these facts were concerns for both because "an angel of the Lord appeared to Zechariah… and told him: "Do not be afraid, Zechariah, for your prayer has been heard, and your wife Elizabeth will bear you a son, and you shall call his name John." [14] And you will have joy and gladness, and many will rejoice at his birth… (1: 13-14).

The Kingdom of God 2

He will be great and will be called the Son of the Most High. And the Lord God will give him the throne of his father David, [33] and he will reign over the house of Jacob forever, and of his kingdom there will be no end" (1: 32-33).

Now, the above story in the Gospel's narrative was happening shortly before Mary was announced to be with a child-a King (1: 33). But when the first time the whole phrase *kingdom of God* is introduced in the Gospel, also, there were oppressions: "there was a man possessed by a demon"; Peter's mother in law was experiencing high fever; and many members of the community were bringing people with various sicknesses to Jesus. As underlined in the table above, the needs assessed at that particular moment included "a spiritual disturbance" and "sickness" (4:33 -41). Therefore, Jesus put into practice some of the manifestations that accompany the "good news"-the kingdom of God-by sending free the one possessed by a demon and healing/curing the sick. These two stories, articulated within the introduction of the theme *kingdom of God* in Luke's story (4: 43), portray Jesus as a model of social activist-searching for joy, gladness, comfort, peace, justice, and righteousness for the common-good of God's people. The events are recorded in this Gospel immediately follow Jesus' words:

"The Spirit of the Lord is on me,
because he has anointed me

to proclaim good news to the poor.

He has sent me to proclaim freedom for the prisoners

and recovery of sight for the blind,

to set the oppressed free,

to proclaim the year of the Lord's favor."

My intention in writing this manuscript is not to provide a solution for every particular problem that we encounter on our way. It is to help us identify the needs of those that God leads to our path and be sensitive to His inner voice, who calls and empowers us to be actively participants in His kingdom-carrying and offering the healing, peace, justice, and righteousness initiated by Jesus in Luke's story. It is my intention that the readers capture a clearer image of what the theme kingdom of God is about, here and now, and maintain hope for the future encounter with the King-Jesus. It will be wise if the readers follow the biblical narrative and, every time the phrase *kingdom of God* appears, perform a hermeneutical study, finding and/or identifying the needs of those individuals, groups, or communities to whom the kingdom of God is presented. Each reader would make their own table with at lease four columns: (1) one to job down the actual needs surrounding the event, (2) one to job down the text in which those needs appear, (3) another one to job down the characters involved in the story/event, and last but not least, (4) the text in which the phrase "kingdom of God" appear. This exercise may create opportunities for one to find more needs, compare them with other readers (during a group study), and present new ways/ideas for advocacy, implementation of justice, and, above all, preaching the good news of the kingdom of God....

The Kingdom of God 3

"I must preach the good news of the kingdom of God to the other towns as well; for I was sent for this purpose" (4: 43).

The events surrounding the presentation of the kingdom of God are full of oppressions, either events that are actually happening at that particular moment (as you may notice or will see ahead), story telling from the past, and even future events. But the main purpose (as Jesus says) is preaching the good news…. This preaching must articulate issues or themes that may bring the audience to consider justice, or to better say, social justice within to good news. Jesus did it! Although it may take some risks, let's see:

I tell you, there were many widows in Israel in the days of Elijah, when the heavens were shut up three years and six months, and a great famine came over all the land, ²⁶ and Elijah was sent to none of them but only to Zarephath, in the land of Sidon, to a woman who was a widow. ²⁷ And there were many lepers in Israel in the time of the prophet Elisha, and none of them was cleansed, but only Naaman the Syrian (4: 24-27).

Jesus underlined *famine* as a community concern, *human identity-* a widow, *leprosy*, and even the *times* in which the events were happening in His preaching. I believe these themes have something to do with social justice. And some times we have to take chances! Let's see what happened to Jesus right after He underlined such facts to the audience:

28 When they heard these things, all in the synagogue were filled with wrath. 29 And they rose up and drove him out of the town and brought him to the brow of the hill on which their town was built, so that they could throw him down the cliff (4: 28-29).

The Kingdom of God 4

"Blessed are you who are poor, for yours is the kingdom of God (6: 20).

The accounts on the kingdom of God continue underlining Jesus choosing his disciples "whom he also named Apostles" (6:13). These apostles were "poor, hungry and weeping "now," and even hated, excluded, revile, and defame on account of the Son of Man." Still, Jesus said to them: "yours is the kingdom of God" (6: 20-26). This saying is not just underlined by Luke but also in Mathew's Gospel in the beatitudes text, where Mathew refers to the kingdom of God as the kingdom of heaven. The passage here in Luke highlights the blessings and the woes- blessings for those to whom Jesus "looked up" and assessed their needs; and expressed a blessing, "yours is the kingdom of God" and owes to "you who are rich for you have received your consolation..." (6: 24). You (the Apostles) are poor, ...hungry [here and now] (in their time), ...weep, ...hate ...excluded ... revile ...defame.... Then Jesus added: "rejoice in that day and leap for joy, for surely your reward is great in heaven." Don't you think it makes sense (if I record Matthew language) when Jesus taught His disciples to pray to say, "Your kingdom come, your will be done on earth as it is in heaven" (Matthew 6:10). On the other hand, in our days, (although social justice may be controversially-defined by Catholics vs. progressives) social justice advocators observe and advocate against oppressive issues that involve what Jesus highlighted above-those who are poor now vs. the rich ones-the ones who are full now, laughing now, and even speak well of them (6: 24-26). This social justice action and/or controversial perspective approach to battle oppression has been happening today at least since the 1840s (https://www.heritage.org/poverty-and-inequality/.../social-justice-not-what-you-think-i...).

The Kingdom of God 5

I tell you, among those born of women none is greater than John. Yet the one who is least in the kingdom of God is greater than he (7: 28).

Oh, how interesting and curious this social justice research is being developed! I almost skip these marvelous facts regarding John the Baptist and his disciples. I was already examining Jesus' disciples' calling, articulating the narrative of chapters 6 through 8, when the Spirit called my attention to take another look into chapter 7 and the first couple of verses of chapter 8. Take a look at the story of when John the Baptist sent messengers to find out *who Jesus was:*

[18] *The disciples of John reported all these things to him. And John,* [19] *calling two of his disciples to him, sent them to the Lord, saying, "Are you the one [u]who is to come, or [v]shall we look for another?"* [20] *And when the men had come to him, they said, "John the Baptist has sent us to you, saying, 'Are you the one [u]who is to come, or [v]shall we look for another?'"* [21] *In that hour he healed many people of diseases and plagues and evil spirits, and[x]on many who were blind he bestowed sight.* [22] *And he answered them, "Go and tell John what you have seen and heard: the blind receive their sight, the lame walk, [z]lepers[5] are cleansed, and [a]the deaf hear, [b]the dead are raised up, [c]the poor have good news preached to them.* [23] *And blessed is the one who is [d]not offended by me."*

[24] *When John's messengers had gone, Jesus[6] began to speak to the crowds concerning John: "What did you go out [e]into the wilderness to*

see? *A reed shaken by the wind? ²⁵ What then did you go out to see?* *A man dressed in soft clothing? Behold, those who are dressed in splendid clothing and live in luxury are in kings' courts. ²⁶ What then did you go out to see? ᵍA prophet? Yes, I tell you, and more than a prophet. ²⁷ This is he of whom it is written,*

ᵇ " Behold, I send my messenger before your face,who will prepare your way before you. ²⁸ I tell you, among those born of women none is greater than John. Yet the one who is least in the kingdom of God is greater than he."

Here is the phrase "the kingdom of God" again, and this time to value every human being member of such kingdom: "the one who is least in the kingdom of God...." Once again, the phrase is accompanied by acts of benevolence and freedom from oppression being performed by Jesus, whether someone likes it or not. Therefore, "blessed is anyone who takes no offense" at Jesus (7: 23). These acts express the *common good* for the members of society. Check this: "*The blind receive their sight, the lame walk, lepers are cleansed, and the deaf hear, the dead are raised up, the poor have good news preached to them (7: 22b).* No matter who they were or where they were in life they were precious and valued by Jesus our King. These acts may not be just miracles or signs that identify Jesus as the promised Savior, but also as a healer, activist, and advocator making a difference in society. This is known in our days as *social justice.* Therefore, the kingdom of God is a social kingdom!

The kingdom of God 6

The good news of the kingdom of God (8:1)

Now, going back to the apostles, … they (the Apostles) were also the first ones called and empowered actively participants of the kingdom of God here and now. They were privileged to know the secrets of the kingdom of God (8:10-11). These were revealed to the apostles by Jesus immediately after Jesus was invited by a Pharisee into his house, and a sinful woman washed his feed with her tears and dried Jesus' feet with her hair (7: 36-50). This act was a preamble for the narrator of the Gospel to introduce the phrase "kingdom of God" one more time. "Soon afterward he went on through cities and villages, proclaiming and bringing the good news of the kingdom of God (8: 1).

Being sin one of the mayor concerns in this writing, let's find out something about this subject:

The narrative in Chapter 7 records about a woman who had lived a sinful life. What does it mean to live a sinful life? Can living a sinful life be considered and issue to be evaluated in order to assess needs in that particular story? Of course! Not just for labeling a person alone for who she/he is or where is in life journey, but her gender, also a woman! Sinful! What did she do to be called "sinful? Now, who was the one that called sinful to this woman? Did Jesus see her as sinful or as a person who needed to be cared for and set free? Can she be an example of a battered woman in the Bible?

The topic of sin or being sinful may be extensive to be exposed, but for now, I am going to explore it by taking a look at the Oxford Dictionary! Later, in chapter 17, sin will be exposed in a personal human experience perspective. According to Oxford the definition of sin or being sinful has to do with wickedness' and immorality committing or characterized by the committing of sins. It is about *a sinful way of life*. Just by examining such a definition, many readers may not be satisfied because of the difference that the word sinful has with the past cultures and what it is here and now and will be in modern times. Can sin be about human nature? Of course! It is about *sinful desires within our own hearts, sinful habits, sinful choices, condemnation of the flesh, sinful actions, and unnatural human corruption.* The biblical narrative records that *"Once Adam disobeyed God, however, we became a fallen and sinful race living in a cursed world."* In other words, sin invades individuals, *"family units as it does all other aspects of society."* But there is always hope! As someone has written:

"The City of Man is a world of profound imperfection, peopled by fallen, sinful beings who can only hope for ultimate citizenship in the City of God through an earthly life of piety."

Therefore, the conscience of sin or being sinful can be very well related to the human hope and the mercy of the one offering the kingdom of God. *"We may believe that His saving work is so effective that there is no sin that cannot be forgiven and no sinner too sinful to be cleansed"* (*https://en.oxforddictionaries.com/definition/sinful*). These are some thoughts that may come to mine when exploring the theme of the sinful woman. Can the needs of that woman be assessed for who she was and did to Jesus? Can the needs of the Pharisees be included? What about Jesus' situation? Do you think this story can be included in this exposition because it happened immediately before the story of the parable of the sower when Jesus told his disciples that to them, it revealed the secrets of the kingdom of God? Well, I just did it!

The kingdom of God 7 and 8

"To you it has been given to know the secrets of the kingdom of God, but for others they are in parables, so that 'seeing they may not see, and hearing they may not understand" (Luke 8:10-11).

"And He sent them out to proclaim the kingdom of God and to perform healing" (9:2, 11).

Although privileged to know the secrets of the kingdom of God, the disciples experienced in their own flesh the struggles faced by any other member of a particular community. As the first participants of the kingdom of God, they received power and authority from Jesus "over demons and to cure diseases" (9:1), and "He sent them out to proclaim the kingdom of God" (9:2). And even though they were poor "now," Jesus instructed them "to take nothing, probably from the littler bit they had, for the journey-no staff, bag, bread, money; not even an extra tunic (9:3). Why? God knows! It may be for welcoming purposes or to create opportunities for others to give, provide, or care for! It could be, also for others to create welcoming environments while the apostles deliver the message of the kingdom (9:5) or vise versa-for the apostles to welcome those who come to hear and receive that message, as Jesus welcomed the crowd who followed Him when the apostles returned from their journey. Jesus took them with him and they withdrew to a town called Bethsaida. According to the text's narrative,

Jesus "welcomed that crowd which followed Him, and spoke to them about the kingdom of God, and healed those who needed healing" (9:11). What a great opportunity!

The kingdom of God 9

"...There are some of those standing here who will not taste death until they see the kingdom of God" (9:27).

Now, after Peter declared that Jesus is the Messiah (9: 18-20), Jesus predicted His death (9: 21-22). This prediction came accompanied by more human oppression: suffering, rejection, even death, and other "social" effects. In other words, the need assessed in Luke's story even temporally affected the King, Jesus. Moreover, Jesus stated from whom that oppression is coming: the elders, chief priests, and the teachers of the law- "The Son of Man must suffer many things and be rejected by the elders, the chief priests and the teachers of the law, and he must be killed..." (9: 22). But everything does not end there! It also comes accompanied by the best "social justice" piece humanity may experience, *life;* an invitation for "all" to enjoy "life": "and on the third day be raised to 'life'" (9:22b); and "Whoever wants to be my disciple must deny themselves and take up their cross daily and follow me" (9: 23).

Now, death may be interpreted by many as the worst part of a person suffering the effects of injustices or nonviolently fighting against injustice! It may be the last fatal experience while advocacy takes place! But, also, (I will say this stamen by faith in my King, Jesus Christ) social justice is or has been guaranteed for "some" before death takes place; check this! "Truly I tell you, some who are standing here (here and now-at that particular time) will not taste death before they see the kingdom of God" (9: 27). Did you get it? Maybe not, because you are not thinking about what I am just thinking! This is what I want to say: "the kingdom of God is a kingdom full of righteousness and justice." Therefore, before some people die, they will rest in peace and be satisfied because justice has taken place for them as members of the kingdom of God. This is just a thought from 9: 27. What else can you get or come up with your mind about the kingdom of God? Can you share it? But remember, anything that we say that is not printed in the biblical text is simply suggestions, expectations and /or comments! It may be just spiritual words that we bring into the text! It may be just sharing thoughts! Thanks for sharing!

The kingdom of God 10

Go and proclaim everywhere the kingdom of God (9: 60).

When the kingdom of God is offered in this Gospel, there was also a lack of resources (intentionally), a need for healing, a lack of food, a lack of dwelling, and, as I had demonstrated, even death suffering (Chapter 9). As it has been written, some of these mentioned pain and stressors were experienced by the apostles (9:3), people from the crowd who fallowed Jesus (9:10; 12-13), Jesus Himself (9:58), and individuals who were also called by Jesus to proclaim the kingdom of God (9:60). The last one is later confirmed in the story of the mission of the seventy, which were seventy others appointed by Jesus and sent ahead of Him proclaiming the kingdom of God and underlining to the audience that "the kingdom of God has come near." The need assessed in this missionary text may be an intentional lack of provisions (although the apostles were poor now) and personal comfort (10:1-12). I use the word "intentionally" do to the fact that the apostles were instructed by Jesus not to take provisions for their journey (9: 3-5), and as a result of that obedience, it could be the case that they may be affected in their personal and/or group comfort. But these are just expectations! Although the kingdom of God is about to be proclaimed one more time!

The kingdom of God 11

The kingdom of God has come near to you... (10: 8-12).

Also, one more time, the kingdom of God is presented in this Gospel's narrative accompanied by healing. Moreover, with awareness words and non-violence protest: "and heal those in it who are sick, and say to them, 'The kingdom of God has come near to you'" (10:8). This is why I sustain that the kingdom of God is full of social justice; and thoughts like the one presented above come to mind. Check this! "But whatever city you enter and they do not receive you, go out into its streets and say, 'Even the dust of your city which clings to our feet we wipe off in protest against you; yet be sure of this, that the kingdom of God has come near'".... It is like to say, "a new down is here and now"! It is not clear that Jesus is instructing his followers to advocate for a righteous, judge, and moral kingdom? The passages seems to indicate that the proclaimers of the kingdom must "protest" with visual, physical, and nonviolent actions against those individuals and even communities who does not welcome a righteous, fear, and justice kingdom: [we] "protest against you; yet be sure of this, that the kingdom of God has come near" (10: 8-12).

The kingdom of God 12 & 13

Your kingdom come (11: 2)!

Then, your kingdom comes! Once again, more oppressions, disadvantages, and anxiety may arise with this next kingdom of God quote. This quote overlaps the story when the disciples asked Jesus to teach them how to pray. In fact, the need for spiritual education, communication or relationship with God is underlined (11:1); and with a petition-"teach us how to pray" (11: 1-13). Therefore, Jesus replied by introducing what is known today as The Lord's Prayer. Here, besides expressing their praise for God, the need for physical bread, and constant forgiveness, Jesus taught his disciples to plea for God's will while articulating a desire for relief of human needs-"Your kingdom come" (11: 2b). Therefore, the prayer lesson of Jesus to His disciples seems to indicate that is based on the need of humanity for a kingdom different than what our world can offer us. Moreover, for a King who can justify, care, and protect those who follow Him.

It is interesting to capture that the narrative of Chapter 11 (where the phrase the kingdom of God is mentioned in Our Father) is linked to the next kingdom of God's phrase in the story of Jesus and Beelzebul by Jesus' motivation about perseverance prayer for those in need, all humanity (5-13). The principle underlined in this link is that when one has nothing, ask, search, and knock- "for everyone who ask receives, and everyone who search finds, and for everyone who knock, the door will be opened" (10). Interesting! I believe I am underlining that every time the phrase, *the kingdom of God,* is mentioned in this Gospel something oppressing is happening, that calls for the identification of needs and the possible solutions for social justice! Jesus is offering that solution and justice-the kingdom of God!

Now, here it comes: Jesus and Beelzebul! This time the human need went as far as the spiritual sphere-when Jesus healed a mute man possessed by a mute demon, casting the demon out (11:14-23). Do you think that his healing occurred by a person representing another kingdom different from the kingdom of God? Do not misjudge! I believe it is clear and transparent! It was done by the active "finger of God" (20) because "the kingdom of God has come to you" (20b). Once again, it is God in action when healing is taking place! Healing is part of the justice demonstrated by Jesus as an action happening within the kingdom of God.

The kingdom of God 14

For it is your Father's pleasure to give you His kingdom (12: 29-32).

As many Puerto Rican say, "wao que detalle" (what a fact)! What a powerful text in relationship to what I am exposing; the needs assessment overlaps the theme of The Kingdom of God, just here in the Gospel of Luke! Please study the text and you may capture some realities inspired by the Holy Spirit (Luke 12: 22-32). The text is about one's worries! Although more needs are identified within it. The passage is about an order of priorities. What is more important life or food, and body or clothing? Now, does the text contradict everything I am writing about? I am performing a need assessment every time the phrase the kingdom of God is mentioned. Now Jesus says do not worry about food and clothing. It is not Jesus Himself concerned about humanity's needs in view to bring justice, healing and common–good for it? It is not Jesus Himself appointing, blessing, and sending His disciples and followers to do the same? Why Jesus is underlining now that food and clothing are not too important? You be the judge! Be careful to misjudge and question God!

Well, once again, the need may be related to food and clothing (22b-23). The need may be for individuals, groups, and/or even nationwide and their concerns. But even though food and clothing do not occupy the firs places in the order of the human priority list, "they are given to you as well" (31) as the ones coming with the things of the kingdom of God-the heavenly things. Are the human needs important for God? "Seguro que yes" (as it is also said by many Puerto Ricans when we use Spanglish and want to affirm something with the word "sure")! It feels great when God take us in His hand and provide for us!

I do not want to leave behind the physical touch of the Lord as part of the healing which comes with the influence of the kingdom of God in human lives. This is in relationship with some of the needs previously mentioned and some others about to come. These are the lack of speech (11:14), physical deformation-a crippled woman (13:11), and abdominal swelling, dropsy (14:2). Here, the manifestation of the relief that comes from the kingdom of God through its participants underlines such human/physical touch. As previously mentioned, (1) the Finger of God (11:20), (2) Jesus' hand (13:13), and (3) Jesus taking hold of someone (14:4). It's that something? What can you get about touching, especially when God inspires that touch? Don't even say what you are thinking if it comes out of context! Yes, sometimes it is risky! But, sometimes, when it is inspired by the Spirit, as risky as it can be, "fountains of living waters may manifest as a result of that touch. The key element here may be that when the Lord touches someone, what comes with His kingdom takes over the pain, suffering, and freedom takes place. May the Lord touch you and heal you here and now!

The kingdom of God 15 & 16 (Luke 13)

Luke 13 contains three more quotes underlining the kingdom of God and some more oppression points, which may inspire one to desire a change even gradually. "…What is **the kingdom of God** like, and to what shall I compare it? It is like a mustard seed…"(13: 18, 19); "…To what shall I compare **the kingdom of God**? It is like leaven…" (13: 20-21); and "…when you see Abraham and Isaac and Jacob and all the prophets in **the kingdom of God**, but yourselves being thrown out. And they will come from east and west and from north and south, and will recline at the table in **the kingdom of God**…" (13: 28-30).

The need assessments that come within those verses have to do with sin, suffering, and encouragement to repentance; otherwise one will perish (2-3). They have to do with spiritual influences that cause illness and the observance of the Sabbath Law (10-17). And questioning salvation could be the greatest need (23). Once again, the Gospel's writer highlights events within the presentation of the kingdom of God that invite its readers to consider social justice to battle human/social and even spiritual concerns or disturbances. Jesus has demonstrated being concerned for society and has advocated for changes, placing the freedom of humanity first before any law that might oppress it! Can we do the same?

The kingdom of God 17

Again, the struggle continues with a mixing of the observance of the Sabbath Law and illness. But also with more manifestation of the healing and affirmation of Jesus about the supremacy that human common-good have over any other thing, the Sabbath Law in this case. Remember, it is not life better than food or body better than clothing! Which is the priority in any given situation? Now it is human health and condition vs. the law of the observance of the Sabbath (13: 10-19). Jesus has demonstrated to me that doing justice for the well-being of others is a priority for the participants of God's kingdom. The case of human situation vs. what can be done or not done on the Sabbath day is so serious and so important to Jesus that He expresses it loud to the crowd and challenges His accusers, publicly, to evaluate the situation of human need. In other words, "you break the Law of the Sabbath to give water to an ox or donkey; why not for a human being? This is what was happening immediately prior to the next quote "kingdom of God" in the biblical narrative, which is "what is the kingdom of God like…"(13: 18)?

The kingdom of God 18

Blessed is everyone who will eat bread in **the kingdom of God** (14: 15-24)!

Also on the Sabbath, Jesus healed the man who had dropsy. Then challenged the hypocrites, I mean, the lawyers and Pharisees, "it is lawful to cure people on the Sabbath, or not?" There was no answer, just silence! So Jesus healed him and sent him away (3-4). Once again, here is another example of the human need as a priority over the Sabbath law: if a child or an ox falls in a well on a Sabbath day, will you not immediately pull it out (5)? Well to Jesus humanity and our condition of human, our needs take priority over any other thing on earth. Jesus cares for all humanity, especially, for those in disadvantages… the poor, the crippled, the lame, and the blind. Can we also practice it? Therefore, blessed is everyone who will eat bread in **the kingdom of God** (14: 15-24)!

The kingdom of God 19

"The Law and the Prophets were proclaimed until John; since that time the gospel of **the kingdom of God** has been preached, and everyone is forcing his way into it…" **(16: 16-17).**

The need assessment now takes a turn into the financial perspective! As in the coming chapter 16, wealth and riches versus lack of sharing resources seem to be a stumbling block for one to participate in the kingdom of God. If a person has more than enough and lacks to share his/her possessions may be at a disadvantage to those who have nothing. In regards to money management, if there is a misuse of riches, and no actions of benevolence by sharing resources with the needed ones, that can be a problem here and now and in the "future" kingdom of God. Now, the needs assessed here are wealth and riches- its management and their lack of sharing with other members of a particular community (16: 1-15; 31; 18: 18-30). In one of the stories or parables, Jesus talks about a shrewd manager. The question may be, is there a problem with entering the kingdom of God because of the misuse of resources or being diligent to be welcomed into an eternal dwelling?

The other story is about Lazarus and the rich man (16: 19-31), which seems to indicate that in a lifetime of receiving "good things" (as the rich man received) and not using them for the common good of others it might be a problem to

45

enjoy the future kingdom (16: 25a). As you may capture later, it may be socially sinful. On the other hand, receiving "evil thing", as Lazarus received (16:25b), seems to be an indication that there will be rest and comfort in the future state of the kingdom of God for those who struggle in our present lifetime and had been ignored by those who received "good things" in the present life. This wake-up call story or parable (as some scholars suggest) is an indication that the kingdom of God is a New Testament thing, which began since John the Baptist; without ignoring the Old Testament [Moses and the prophets]. According to the biblical narrative here, everyone tries to enter the kingdom of God by force (16:16).

The kingdom of God 20

Sin

Sin, what is sin? While writing this section, I admit that I am writing in fear, but at the same time assured of what I am about to print ahead. I admit that I am a sinner; a sinner reconciled with God by the work of my Savior Jesus Christ, my King. I admit that my *free act* of sin has affected my inner life and relationship with God and my neighbor. Sin has affected my life and relationship with my family and friends, relatives, church, and community in which I have lived, and, even, it might have been an addition to the worldly statistics numbers in various areas where family, church, and society had been impacted by a changed. What I mean to say is that *sin* in its theological aspect affects *the freedom* of the inheritance of the kingdom of God. The inheritance of the kingdom needs unconditional forgiveness in order to shed light on the redemptive work of King Jesus Christ; but in its humanistic sense, as John Paul II sustains, all *"sin is social."*

Sin is identified here as one of "the other disciples" oppressed needs assessment (17:6). Not only that! Jesus commanded the apostles to "rebuke"… but "forgive" *unconditionally*, not everyone else, but exclusively *other disciples* [members of the kingdom of God] dealing with sin. This fact does not mean that the principles of unconditional forgiveness cannot be applied to the rest of the world; or to inclusively say, *these litter ones* (17:6).

47

Freedom of sin

As it has been stated above, sin affects the freedom of humanity and resounds socially! Even though sin has created such great consequences in my life, church, and society, sin is not problematic for me! I do not live preoccupied with sin. Sinning is part of my everyday life. Although, I do not go on sinning for God's grace to increase! I am certainly sure that God has credited me with life-long forgiveness through the redemptive work of Jesus Christ my King. I am free in Christ because, in Christ, I believe! If Jesus died for my sins why worry about sin? I believe in the New Covenant sealed with the precious blood of my King- Jesus Christ. Why living preoccupied with sin? In God's perspective, I died on the cross with Christ; There is and will be no law that has dominium over the members of the kingdom who have died on the cross with Jesus; therefore sin is dead; Christ's life has been credited back to us; we live by faith; and God consider us alive in Christ. Let's see some of the texts that the biblical narrative records about sin:

"Do you not know, brothers and sisters—for I am speaking to those who know the law—that the law has authority over someone only as long as that person lives? 2 For example, by law a married woman is bound to her husband as long as he is alive, but if her husband dies, she is released from the law that binds her to him. 3 So then, if she has sexual relations with another man while her husband is still alive, she

is called an adulteress. But if her husband dies, she is released from that law and is not an adulteress if she marries another man.

4 So, my brothers and sisters, you also died to the law through the body of Christ, that you might belong to another, to him who was raised from the dead, in order that we might bear fruit for God. 5 For when we were in the realm of the flesh,[a] the sinful passions aroused by the law were at work in us, so that we bore fruit for death. 6 But now, by dying to what once bound us, we have been released from the law so that we serve in the new way of the Spirit, and not in the old way of the written code. 7 What shall we say, then? Is the law sinful? Certainly not! Nevertheless, I would not have known what sin was had it not been for the law. For I would not have known what coveting really was if the law had not said, "You shall not covet."[b] 8 But sin, seizing the opportunity afforded by the commandment, produced in me every kind of coveting. For apart from the law, sin was dead.

(Romans 7:1-8 NIV)

20 I have been crucified with Christ and I no longer live, but Christ lives in me. The life I now live in the body, I live by faith in the Son of God, who loved me and gave himself for me. 21 I do not set aside the grace of God, for if righteousness could be gained through the law, Christ died for nothing!"

(Galatians 2:20-21 NIV)

2 Set your minds on things above, not on earthly things. 3 For you died, and your life is now hidden with Christ in God. 4 When Christ, who is your life, appears, then you also will appear with him in glory.

(Colossians 3:2-4 NIV)

1 In the same way, count yourselves dead to sin but alive to God in Christ Jesus.

(Romans 6:11 NIV)

As it has been said, *"God's perspective is the only one that counts in eternity. As far as He is concerned you have already paid the price for your sins even though someone else experienced the agony of the execution. God "imputed" the punishment of the cross, to your account as if you had actually been condemned to die there. God considers all the sins you've committed and all the sins you will commit in the future as "paid for." You have already died, once--and that was enough to terminate the law's dominance over your life. Therefore, sin and the law that empowers it no longer has dominion over your life! Sin no longer has the power to condemn (Romans 8:1-4)--it no longer has the power to project guilt when you know the truth. The only thing God requires from a Christian who has committed sin is acknowledgement. John 1:9 tells us that if we confess our sins, he is faithful and just to forgive us our sins, and to cleanse us from all unrighteousness. When we sin--we confess it immediately to God, get up and keep going as if the sin never happened. This is the good news of the gospel."*

(http://www.rockofoffence.com/oppress1.html)

The good news for the members of the kingdom of God in regard to sin is clearly recorded in the following verse: *"For sin shall no longer be your master, because you are not under the law, but under grace" (Romans 6:14 NIV).*

Sin is Social

All sin is social because, as the famous English poet John Donne said, "no man (and woman) is an island. Every individual is part of the continent, but in this specific work, the kingdom of God is not just for only one person. There are also other members of the kingdom that together with Christ compose the society of the kingdom of God and, temporally, the earthly society. This is to say and I underlined it above, that sin wounds neighbor/humans' relationship. This is not about blaming external factors of society for one's personal sinful act. Yes, sin is a personal act. It is a freedom action of an individual, not of a group or a community. In other words, society does not and cannot sin, but each particular individual in it can, and others suffer the consequences of sin! The king that lives in others is wounded by all individuals' sins! These individuals may be motivated to freely sin by numerous and powerful external factors and/or defects or habits articulated with the human condition. In other words, only the individual alone is responsible for sin. And sin is social for its effects. It resonates in the individual, others, the church, and the whole terrestrial world. All these parties suffer the consequences of all sin.

"Also social is every sin against the common good and its exigencies in relation to the whole broad spectrum of the rights and duties of citizens. The term social can be applied to sins of commission or omission—on the part of political, economic or trade union leaders, who though in a position to do so, do not work diligently and wisely for the improvement and transformation of society according to the requirements and potential of the given historic moment; as also on the part of workers who through absenteeism or non-cooperation fail to ensure that their industries can continue to advance the well-being of the workers themselves, of their families and of the whole of society.

An employer sins against the common good when he fails to pay a just wage....

(John Paul II).

As readers may perceive and understand, sin may be or can be a mayor oppressor without foundation in today's date for the members of the kingdom of God and those who are called to enter into it. Sin has many individuals bound into it when God has granted freedom in the person of Jesus Christ. Many Individuals sin and their social connection suffer it effects and/or consequences. Rebuking and unconditional forgiveness must be actively taking place for one's faith strengthening and the kingdom of God, as a mustard seed (17:6; 13:19), gradually develops and grows until our King Jesus returns. We, the members of the kingdom of God are free for interacting within society to do good work.

"For we are God's handiwork, created in Christ Jesus to do good works, which God prepared in advance for us to do."

(Ephesians 2: 10 NIV)

The kingdom of God 21

... 'The kingdom of God is not coming... is in your midst" (17: 20-21)

Suffering and rejection

The suffering and rejection were experimented on by Jesus, The Son of Man Himself (17:25). This generation experiments on them also! I underline suffering and rejection as the next need assessed here because in one way or another humanity is a partaker of them. People suffer and get hurt and they can make other people suffer and hurt. Humanity experiences the pain caused by suffering and rejection. The biblical narrative seems to indicate that suffering and rejection is a preamble of distinction of the kingdom of God to any other kingdom that may be offered in this world. The kingdom that comes accompanied with rest, compassion, and tender love "is in your midst" (17:21b) - although humans experience suffering, pain, and rejection temporarily. Therefore many Christians agree with the message drawn from the following verse:

"The coming of the kingdom of God is not something that can be observed, 21 nor will people say, 'here it is,' or 'there it is,' because the kingdom of God is in your midst"

(17:20-21 NIV).

Can you see it? Can you feel it? Can you experience it?

It seems to me that the phrase "the kingdom of God is in your midst" is because Jesus Christ the King was there! Although experiencing suffering in His human sense and rejection for being human and divine, the kingdom of God was in that particular moment, as it is today, in your (our) midst! If one looks at the definition of the word "human being" one can find out that it relates to *"a man, woman, or child of the species Homo sapiens, distinguished from other animals by superior mental development, power of articulate speech, and upright stance. Yet these are* **human beings** *like you and me, people who think and feel, who hurt and can be hurt"*

(https://en.oxforddictionaries.com/definition/human_being). If this is true, as many of us have experienced in our lifetime, there is no dough that Jesus suffered and has been rejected in deed been him "the kingdom of God."

The kingdom of God 22 (Luke 18: 15-17)

"…'Permit the children to come to Me, and do not hinder them, for **the kingdom of God** belongs to such as these. Truly I say to you, whoever does not receive **the kingdom of God** like a child will not enter it at all'" (Luke 18:15, 16, 17).

Lack of justice, faith and self-pride

The kingdom of God is about justice for the injustice suffering ones. It is not about self-pride nor own righteousness although both can be good things. Pride and righteousness in themselves are not bad things and can be very useful for maintaining living standards. However, when it is about feeling superior or better than others, both are deadly sinful thoughts/actions. Therefore they are identified here as oppressed issues.

The kingdom of God is about humbleness when exaltation is self-intended. It is about exaltation when humbleness takes place. The partakers of the kingdom must be faithful diligent advocates of justice for the oppressed ones (18:1-8 NIV). They must create a welcoming atmosphere for the kingdom of God to come and be experienced by others–*as welcoming a child* (18: 15-17 NIV). This is where the verse "Permit the children to come to Me, and do not hinder them, for **the kingdom of God** belongs to such as these" may applied. Therefore, the needs assessed which relate to justice, faith, and self-pride are addressed by Jesus to the disciples using figurative language or figure of speech (18: 1-17).

The kingdom of God 23

Lack of Sharing (18:18-30; 29-30)

"…How hard it is for those who are wealthy to enter **the kingdom of God**! For it is easier for a camel to go through the eye of a needle than for a rich man to enter **the kingdom of God**'…" (Luke 18:18-27)

"…There is no one who has left house or wife or brothers or parents or children, for the sake of **the kingdom of God**…'" (18: 28-29)

The lack of sharing (giving) can be oppressed for both the one who does not share (especially rich or wealthy individuals) and the one who does not receive from those called to share *the poor* in this case. In other words, there is an oppressive sharing gap that may prevent wealthy individuals from "having treasures in heaven" (22b). The gap just mentioned can be filled by a gift, being generous, and implementing charity. This is by the transfer of something to someone without the expectation of receiving a reward; by creating a habit of giving freely without envisioning receiving something in return; and by practicing giving with the intention to help those in need, especially if the person is not related to the giver. All these giving/sharing practices are key elements for the members of the kingdom of God. Furthermore, this seems to be a command of Jesus to the wealthy ones (22) and those who receive good things in this life. Furthermore, for those who have left their homes, wife, children and "all that they have" to follow the one King Jesus, there are promises-receiving more here and now, and "eternal life in the age to come": "there is no one who has left house or wife or brothers or parents or children, for the sake of the kingdom of God, who will not receive many times more in this time, and in the age to come eternal life" (18: 29-30).

The kingdom of God 24

…the kingdom of God was going to appear immediately (19: 11-27).

Growing disorder

Should I call growing disorder this "next need" if it is really a need at all for a short normal person? Yes, it could be normal or in the normal order for Zacchaeus the fact that he was short in stature; and because of that he could not see who Jesus was (19:3). Was Jesus concerned about Zacchaeus being short? I don't think so! Jesus does not seem to be concerned about individual differences! Why should I? But Jesus seems to be concerned when people are at a disadvantage to others and are treated disrespectfully. Does Zacchaeus complain about being different to other people in the crowd? Did Zacchaeus see himself being short as a problem? It does not look like a problem for him, but a challenging opportunity to strategically reach out to what he wanted…! Apparently, his curiosity motivated him to find a way to fix what others might see as a problem. From a human perspective, he found his strategic way to have an encounter with the King, which without expecting it led him to have a one-on-one with the kingdom of God; not by force, but by the calling of Jesus. The stature of Zacchaeus does not need to be assessed. Instead, it was associated with the fact that he wanted to see who Jesus was. And following the line previously mentioned about the rich man,

Zacchaeus wanted to give or share [of his resources] to others, "here and now"(8), …practicing what seems to be one of the duties of the inheritances of the kingdom-justice. (19: 1-11). This happened near Jerusalem where some (maybe from the crowd, 18: 36) supposed that the kingdom of God was going to appear immediately (19:11). In response to such belief, Jesus continued making history by expressing Himself in parables.

The kingdom of God 25

"...Blessed is The King who comes in the name of the Lord..." (19: 37-38)

"...when you see these things happening, recognize that **the kingdom of God** is near..." (21: 29-33)

Oppressive nearly final world events

The next time that the phrase "kingdom of God" is mentioned in the Gospel (although the word kingdom is mentioned in 19: 37-38) comes full of "oppressive conditions and nearly final worldly events. These are Poverty, war, uprisings (resistance, rebellion, revolt), natural disasters, famines, pestilences, persecution, imprisonment, betrayal, death, and hate. Here a story about the widow's offering vs. the rich's gift into the temple treasury is told. Also, what is expected to happen prior to and during the events near the final times is underlined in this section (21:1-31). Finally, the parable of the fig tree, which is the figurative language used by Jesus to confirm that the kingdom of God is near is about to close the chapter (31). But this would not happen without Jesus' advice about "hearts weighed down with carousing, drunkenness and the anxieties of life, and [that] that day will close on [one] you suddenly like a trap." As the Bible readers may capture once again, every time the kingdom of God is announced by Jesus, there are certain kinds of oppressions experienced by the audience to which

He is addressing the message. Because of the magnitude of these writings, it will be impossible for me to underline each one of them. However, each one of them could be considered as a call for social justice, advocacy and faith-based social action toward a common-good change. Each of them may be included in what follows:

Poverty

Defining poverty may not be a simple saying or a difficult task to understand! Defining poverty may bring some labeling thinking into our minds who is poor and who isn't? It may create margins of distinction to capture the idea of what is being poor. Defining poverty may bring us some past experiences and memories to remember. What is poverty? Poverty has to do with quality and quantity, inferiority and insufficiency. Moreover, poverty is about experience; an experience that bears understanding. Have you ever, imaginarily, placed yourself in somebody else shoes? Let's do that exercise now! Think that you are poor! You live in poverty. You are experiencing:

- An unmet need and an unfulfilled longing.
- A lack of food, shelter, and everything good.
- Being sick and unable to see a doctor.
- Not having an opportunity to go to school; not knowing how to read and write.
- Wearing clothes that do not fit you.
- The fact of standing on the outside looking in.

- Drinking dirty water that you must drink.
- Being without a job and you and your family have no home.
- Walking a long walk without shoes.
- A terrible illness without insurance and a way to treat it.
- Just a "simple" pain in the stomach.
- Vulnerability to every scheme, lie, and cheat.
- Living in a house with an empty refrigerator or having no refrigerator at all; no stove, no electricity.
- Living in a place with one toilet for one hundred neighbors.
- Having a thief in the night or living with a drunken father.
- Having a child lost to preventable disease.
- A mother weeping.
- Injustice without appeal.
- Cruelty, stress, shame, famine, war, pain uprisings (resistance, rebellion, revolt), natural disasters, pestilences, persecution, imprisonment, betrayal, death, and hate,
- Life without life.
- Being marginalize, suffocate, and oppressed.

In fact, poverty kills! (www.fivetalents.org/poverty). It is receiving "evil things", as Lazarus received it. It is having no rest and being comforted in this present life. Poverty is one to be ignored by those who receive "good things" here and now- as the rich man received them (16:25b). Poverty is like not being the rich man who put his gift into the temple treasury; and like being the widow of that story (21: 1-4). Poverty is like not being Zaccheaus-the tax collector (19:8). In conclusion, poverty is not being a member of the kingdom of God, although life experiences have shown to many of us that there is no guarantee to be excluded from the poverty described above.

The kingdom of God 26

"…I shall never again eat it until it is fulfilled in **the kingdom of God**…I will not drink of the fruit of the vine from now on until **the kingdom of God** comes…" (Luke 22:14-23)

"…just as My Father has granted Me **a kingdom**, I grant you that you may eat and drink at My table in **My kingdom**…" (Luke 22:28, 29, 30)

Betrayal, dispute, and trials

Jesus continues announcing the kingdom of God and this time the need assessment in the panorama has to do with betrayal, dispute, and trials (22). I thought: Should I include these three as needs assessed in search for social justice or a social justice solution for all the needs previously presented? Here is the case of Judas who *betrayed* Jesus; the *dispute* among Jesus' disciples, arguing who was considered to be the greatest; and Jesus' trials and suffering. As one may notice, the list of the needs being assessed continues and it seems to overlap with the experience of poverty.

Let's consider betrayal as a short word for the breaking of confidence, which in turn affects the moral and psychological sphere in a relationship. Let's consider betrayal in regard to the work of the members of the kingdom of God. Is betrayal a need assessed while social justice is forthcoming with the kingdom of God? It is not moreover an act that triggered the salvation of those who were about to enter the kingdom of God. Let us be honest in this! Today betrayal breaks relationships. Many of us have experienced that! Being this true, sure, it may be a highlighted painful need for those crying for social justice to take place! But in the case of Judas, do you think that the act of betrayal (Judas to Christ) served as a relationship stumbling block for the whole of humanity or just among the two? As in the case of sin previously discussed, either way, betrayal is social! Remember, "No man is an island."

Now, looking at betrayal through the lens of ethics and then looking at it from the human eye, the fact that Judas betrayed Jesus was a good thing. Did Judas know that Jesus was the Christ prior to the betrayal? In the human sense, Did Judas understand that it was necessary that someone needed to turn Jesus to the Roman authorities for Jesus to be crucified and save the world? Was Judas obeying the voice of the Lord (although satan entered into him) when said, "what you are about to do, do quickly" (John 13:27)? On the other hand, Did Jesus know that he was about to be betrayed by Judas? Did he know that the act of betrayal would take Him to the cross, be crucified, and save the world? Did Jesus know that He was the savior, the king whose kingdom was offered to the world? These are questions that may be interesting to be studied. Also, Judas' questions are Gnostic thinking; "praise of Judas for his role in triggering humanity's salvation and viewing Judas as the best of the apostles!"

Well, humanly speaking there were (maybe) ways to "capture" Jesus to be sentenced to death…. If there were other ways, and not by the participation of Jesus' disciples (Judas in this case), humanly saying, that God was out of control of things that happened on earth and the world took over by "capturing" Jesus to be sent to the cross. The Judas vs. Jesus betraying case is controversial and fear of being judged. Actually, what I just wrote I wrote it under reverence-fear, respecting and honoring my King. But certainly, I hope that the Spirit would illuminate us…! There is no room in this writing to expose Judas' betraying subject. There is no room to talk about Judas' betraying kiss, the actual betrayal act, the 30 silver coins, and Judas' death. Was Judas a member of the kingdom of God? If he was, does he remain in it or was he rejected for his betrayal act and even for the way of death? Were his sins forgiven with the death of Christ? Were his sins social? There may be long controversial writing about this subject and his place among the twelve "best disciple" who set in motion for Jesus' *trials,* crucifixion, and resurrection for the salvation of humanity. There is no room within this writing to talk about that!

The kingdom of God 27

"...a man from Arimathea, a city of the Jews, who was waiting for **the kingdom of God**..." (Luke 23: 50-52).

Decision-making and actions

This next need underlines various factors: the burial of Jesus-death, the position of Joseph of Arimathea; Council member; and his disappointment in front of a decision that he did not consent to; last but not least, Joseph's character (Chapter 23). Although it was what it is! Jesus dies for our sins! Now, the disciples, Jesus' followers, and/or many members of the community may be oppressed. Jesus the King was dead. Joseph came from the town of Arimathea (53b). He himself was waiting for the kingdom of God (53c). But one possible oppressed point was that being a member of the Council (52), he did not consent to their decision and actions [against Jesus] (52b). Do you think that anxiety, frustration, and anger could take place in his life? What were his feelings, emotions, and sensations? Which are yours while hearing these facts?

Now, you may ask, what happened to the other members of the Council? Were they evil? If so, what a good and upright man was doing among evil leaders? Why he did not consent to their decision and actions? Did he understand that the King must die at the hands of criminals? If he was a member of the Council, and that was a body, working as a body (it was supposed to), should the unanimous decision and action include him, as if he consented to it unanimously? Would you count his voice and vote among that of the Council? On the other hand, can righteousness and goodness be oppressing? Can goodness and uprightness count in the needs assessment? If not, Why not if sometimes one is oppressed, feared, and persecuted for advocating for the common good? Think about those community or world leaders who have been killed for being upright and advocating for justice and human rights! Think about our King Jesus Christ, who died, was buried, and rose among the dead for our salvation, freedom, and enjoyment in His kingdom!

The kingdom of God 28

"And he was saying, 'Jesus, remember me when You come in **Your kingdom**!' And He said to him, 'Truly I say to you, today you shall be with Me in Paradise'" (Luke 23: 42-43).

Identity, Arguments/manipulation

Now, the oppressed needs turn or articulate various subjects: identity, manipulation, tax exercise accusation, and questioning about Jesus' kingship. How would you feel about tax exercise, especially while living and working in America? According to Bruce Drake (2014), when April 15 comes, in the United States of America 34% workers in America liked or loved to file their taxes! Of course the other 56% do not like that exercise; 26% hate doing their taxes; 52%-42% believe that their taxes are too high; 57 % feel that the wealthy don't pay their fair share; and 59% "Americans say that so much is wrong with the tax system that Congress should completely change it." Finally, the tax collector itself, the IRS, does not make Americans feel warm all over- 51% expressed unfavorable view of the tax system while 44% regarded it positively (www.pewresearch.org/fact-tank/.../on-tax-day-americans-views-of-taxes-and-the-irs/). Therefore, taxes might be oppressive! By the way, tax exercise was one of the accusations against our King. While Jesus was going through trial, he was accused of opposing payment of taxes to Caesar and claims to be Messiah, a king" (23:3). Think about that! If Jesus were one of the interviewed persons in the research about taxes in the 2014, what would be His perspective about taxes? Would He be advocating for fairness within the tax system? Well, theologically speaking He is! Every time a person or a Christian-faith-based group advocate for... Christ is advocating with them! Which would be Christ's feelings? Would He be count with the 59% that suggest that the system is so wrong or the 51% that is unfavorable to it? What else can you say...? Can taxes be oppressive? Can tax exercise be a cause for a person's dead? Moreover, were there reasons to put a person to die for saying that he is a king? Do you think that Jesus died because of what he did, did not do or for what he said...? Do you think that he died for human reasons, accusations, or sentence? If you think so, you have to meet Jesus again! You have to meet my King! You have to meet that one who even after dead fights against spiritual/human oppressions, and for the common-good of the inheritance of His kingdom!

Thou, the two accusations to Jesus are related to what I have been exposing social justice in the gospel, and the kingdom of God; its principles as a way of salvation in Christ to humanity, which in turn serves as an alternative to human/spiritual oppressions. What coming ahead underlines the identity factor of our King Jesus, which comes to a scene full of manipulation-"If you are this, why don't you do that?" I am very sure you relate yourself with sayings like that one. "If you are a policeman, why are you breaking the law"? If you are a Pastor why your kids are the way they are? These facts may be an indication that people's identity may be the basis for oppression. In this case, Jesus' identity as a King, "led him to death" (although the story did not end there. He is risen, He lives); and his mother, relatives, disciples, and followers to suffer the consequences. So, let's look at how the identity factor moves through some verses of Chapter 23, the final one to be studied in this manuscript:

So Pilate asked Jesus, "Are you the king of the Jews?" "You have said so," Jesus replied (verse 3).

The soldiers also came up and mocked him. They offered him wine vinegar **37** and said, "If you are the king of the Jews, save yourself."**38** There was a written notice above him, which read: this is the king of the Jews.

39 One of the criminals who hung there hurled insults at him: "Aren't you the Messiah? Save yourself and us!" **40** But the other criminal rebuked him. "Don't you fear God," he said, "since you are under the same sentence? **41** We are punished justly, for we are getting what our deeds deserve. But this man has done nothing wrong." **42** Then he said, "Jesus, remember me when you come into your kingdom." **43** Jesus answered him, "Truly I tell you, today you will be with me in paradise."

The main goal in providing the above verses is not to preach another sermon of my call to ministry and the preaching of the gospel. I will let the Spirit reveal it to you! The idea has been to identify those oppression points throughout a needs assessment in this gospel every time that the kingdom of God is underlined or presented in it. Once again, the need has been related but not limited to fear, language development, shame, spiritual disturbance, illness, hunger, disability, poverty, weeping, hater, exclusion, verbal abuse, rejection, lack of resources, lack of food, dwelling, and personal comfort, death, lack of spiritual education and speech, physical differences, bodily discomfort, disability, and pain, wealth, riches misuse, and lack of sharing, sin, suffering, lack of justice and faith, pride, growing differences, war, uprisings, natural disasters, famines, pestilences, persecution, imprisonment, betrayal, and as for Jesus Christ the King, *identity and culture*. As it has been demonstrated, there is a human reason to express, "thy kingdom come" (Mathew 6: 10 KJV) or "Come, Lord Jesus" (Revelation 22: 20b KJV). Amen.

www.ingramcontent.com/pod-product-compliance
Lightning Source LLC
Chambersburg PA
CBHW070933120626
46546CB00004B/1405